RAINFOREST
ANIMALS

written by D Alderton
illustrated by S Boni *and* L R Galante

Ladybird

CONTENTS

WHAT IS A RAIN FOREST?

The world's rain forests grow round the central part of the Earth, in the **tropics**. Rain forests are hot and humid places, but little sunlight passes down through the dense cover of trees and vines to the ground. Here, it is quite dark and there are lots of shadows.

Where are the rain forests?

Rain forests cover about one tenth of the world's surface, but they are home to nine out of ten of the world's plants and animals.

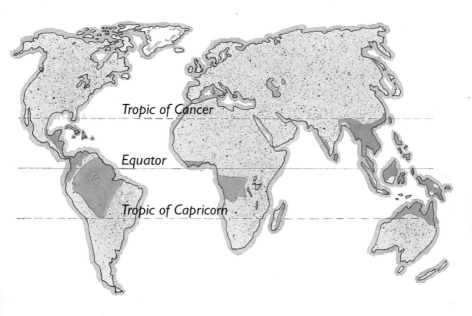

Rain forests are found in the hottest parts of the Earth – between the Tropic of Cancer and the Tropic of Capricorn. In this equatorial region there are no seasons. The weather is always hot and humid. It always becomes dark, quickly, at about 6 pm, every day of the year. The main rain forests are found in the Americas, Africa and Asia. They are the green parts of the map.

THE WATER CYCLE

If you fly over a rain forest in a plane, the forest below will look like a green carpet. There are no seasons here, and the trees have leaves and fruit throughout the year. When it rains, water drips down through the dense **canopy** into the lower parts of the rain forest.

Water everywhere

Rain forests are very wet places. It rains almost every day. But the clouds clear quickly and then it becomes sunny. There is a lot of water **vapour** in the air. This is why being in a rain forest feels sticky. The Sun's heat dries up some of the rain, which then forms clouds. These clouds will produce more rain, and so the water cycle continues.

PLANTS

Some of the most unusual plants in the world grow in the rain forests. More than a quarter of the medicines we use today first came from rain forest plants, along with many of the fruits we eat, like bananas. A number of other plants from the world's rain forests, such as begonias, have found their way into our homes as houseplants.

Rafflesia's giant blooms
The rafflesia produces the largest flowers of any plant in the world. These can measure one metre across, and smell like rotten meat.

Lianas
These are woody
vines which use the
trees like a scaffold
to climb up, clinging
on with tendrils.
Some lianas are thin,
others are thick and
as strong as a rope.

Rosy periwinkle
This plant grows in Madagascar,
off Africa, and is used to help
cure leukaemia, a type of cancer.

9

CREEPY CRAWLIES

No one knows how many insects and similar creatures live in the rain forests of the world. A large number, especially those whose home is up in the forest canopy, have still to be discovered. Some scientists believe there could be as many as 50 million different animals living in the canopy of trees.

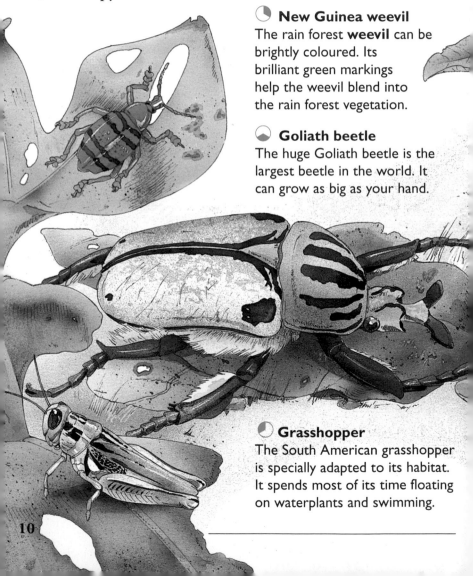

New Guinea weevil
The rain forest **weevil** can be brightly coloured. Its brilliant green markings help the weevil blend into the rain forest vegetation.

Goliath beetle
The huge Goliath beetle is the largest beetle in the world. It can grow as big as your hand.

Grasshopper
The South American grasshopper is specially adapted to its habitat. It spends most of its time floating on waterplants and swimming.

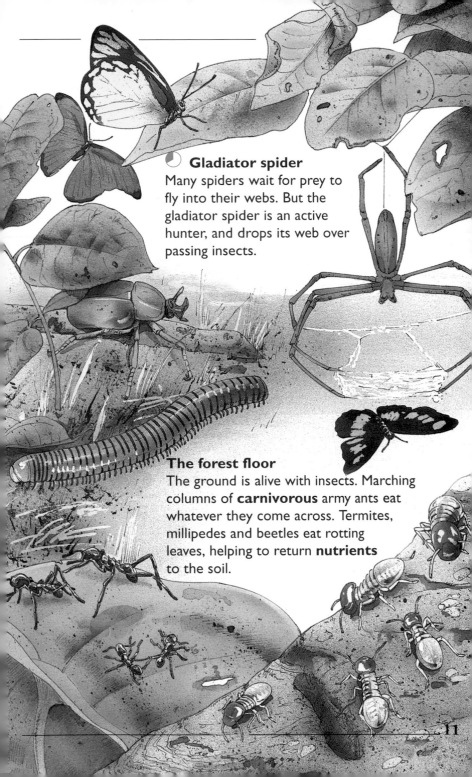

Gladiator spider

Many spiders wait for prey to fly into their webs. But the gladiator spider is an active hunter, and drops its web over passing insects.

The forest floor

The ground is alive with insects. Marching columns of **carnivorous** army ants eat whatever they come across. Termites, millipedes and beetles eat rotting leaves, helping to return **nutrients** to the soil.

FISH

The rivers and streams in rain forests contain fish of many different shapes and sizes. Fish face many enemies, and not all are in the water. Fishing bats, for example, can even locate fish from the air and use a special toe which is shaped like a hook to lift fish out of water.

 Piranha

The piranha is the most feared fish of the Amazon rain forest. The piranha is **predatory**, and feeds on flesh. If an animal is injured, the scent of blood in water will attract large numbers of piranhas to it.

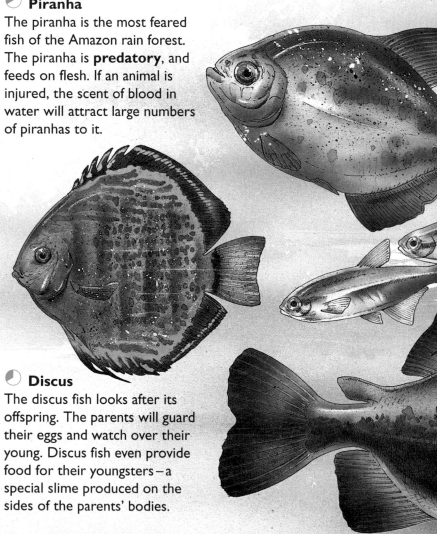

 Discus

The discus fish looks after its offspring. The parents will guard their eggs and watch over their young. Discus fish even provide food for their youngsters—a special slime produced on the sides of the parents' bodies.

Hatchetfish

This fish uses powerful **fins** at the sides of its body to fly short distances above the surface of the water, especially to escape danger.

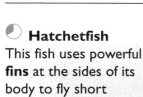

Neon tetra

This fish is so-called because its colours are very bright, like those of a neon sign. It only grows to four centimetres in length, and lives in **shoals**. The neon tetra is a very popular aquarium fish, bred in large numbers round the world.

Angelfish

This fish lives in slow-flowing rivers. The flattened angelfish body shape allows it to swim easily between waterplants. The angelfish is **camouflaged**.

Pacu

The pacu is a relative of the dreaded piranha, but rather than eating meat, the pacu uses its teeth to crush the fruits and seeds which fall off trees that overhang the river.

FROGS, TOADS, LIZARDS AND CROCODILES

Frogs thrive in the moist surroundings of the rain forest. Here, some frogs no longer **spawn** in water, but lay their eggs in leaves, where the eggs are kept moist. A number of interesting **reptiles** have also adapted to rain forest life.

Slender-snouted crocodile
This lives in the rivers of West Africa. It eats fish, **amphibians**, snakes, crabs and shrimps. The crocodile's narrow snout shows that this reptile is not a threat to people.

Horned toad
This toad's shape and colour blend in with the floor covering.

Skink
A skink is a lizard with very short limbs and so it sometimes looks like a snake. The skink feeds mainly on insects.

Flying dragon lizard

Poison arrow frog
The bright colours of this frog warn other animals that it is poisonous. The Choco Indians use the frog's poison to make arrows with poisonous tips.

SNAKES

Snakes can be seen anywhere in the rain forest, from the canopy down to the floor and in the rivers too. The sensitive, forked tongues of these reptiles help them to find their prey. Poisonous snakes have grooved teeth which inject poison. Boas squeeze their prey to death.

Tree viper
This snake hides away during the day and starts to hunt at dusk. It can leap off the ground, when striking at prey – a lizard, frog or small **rodent**.

Emerald tree boa
The colour of this snake changes dramatically as it grows larger. A young emerald tree boa is reddish-orange at first, rather than green.

Bushmaster
This is one of the biggest, poisonous snakes in the world. A single bite can kill a person. Bushmasters often hide in or near the roots of trees.

RAIN FOREST LAYERS

The tallest trees in the rain forest are called emergents. These trees can grow as tall as 35 metres, which is as tall as a twenty-storey building. The uppermost layer is called the canopy.

Trees which make up the forest canopy have long, bare trunks with branches at the top. Most of the treetops form a roof-like layer which prevents sunlight from reaching the forest floor.

Under the thick canopy, there is just enough light for smaller trees and ferns to grow. This layer is called the **understorey**.

The floor of the forest is covered with a layer of fallen leaves, mosses, fungi and dead wood.

OTHER RAIN FOREST ANIMALS

It is often difficult to see animals in the rain forest, even when they are quite big. This is partly why new animals are still being discovered here. The rain forest is also dense, which means that it can be both difficult and dangerous to walk far into the forest, because you could end up lost.

◗ **Lemur**

This strange monkey-like animal lives only on the island of Madagascar, which is near the tip of Africa.

◗ **Okapi**

A relative of the giraffe, the okapi was not discovered until 1901. The okapi feeds on plants in the rain forest, and is hard to spot, in spite of its large size. It is about as tall as a person.

◗ **Capybara**

A capybara is a large rodent and related to a guinea pig. Capybaras live near to water and feed on plants.

TURTLES AND TORTOISES

Tortoises live on the forest floor and eat the fallen fruit and plants found here. Turtles may spend much of their time in rivers and streams. They tend to be carnivorous, and eat creatures like worms and fish. Turtles and tortoises lay eggs, just like birds and other reptiles.

Red-footed tortoise
This tortoise can grow as long as your arm. It is hunted and eaten by people in the forest and faces few other enemies. Some red-footed tortoises have very brightly coloured feet.

Spiny turtle
The sharp spines around the edge of the shell of this turtle are thought to protect it from snakes. It spends some of its time in water, but also wanders on land, finding fruit to eat.

AMAZON RIVER TURTLE

*This turtle grows to a large size, weighing more than a fully-grown person. It lays its eggs on **sandbanks**, when the water level in rivers is low. The young turtles hatch quickly, in a few weeks, before the area is flooded again.*

BIRDS

Most of the thousands of different rain forest birds live in the canopy where there is plenty of food for them to eat – fruit, nuts, flowers and insects. The trees can also be used as nesting sites. Rain forest birds are usually brightly coloured, but their plumage blends in with the background, making birds hard to see in their natural surroundings.

◐ **Macaw**
The macaw is the biggest of all the world's 330 kinds of parrot.

◐ **Toucan**
The toucan's bright and distinctive bill hides its long, feather-like tongue. The bill has a honeycomb structure and is light but strong. The toucan's long bill allows it to pick fruits which otherwise could be out of reach.

Parrot
A parrot uses its strong, hooked beak to crack nuts. It holds food in one claw, then bites into the food.

Hummingbird
The hummingbird is the smallest bird in the world. It can beat its wings so fast that it can **hover** like a helicopter. It is the only bird that can fly backwards.

Bird of paradise
A male bird of paradise uses his magnificent plumage to show off to females in special display areas in the forest. The loud calls of the males attract the females.

Hoatzin
The hoatzin is one of the most primitive of all living birds. A young hoatzin hatches with claws on its wings. A hoatzin eats leaves and shoots.

RAIN FOREST CATS

Several wild cats live in the world's rain forests. Wild cats have good eyesight and hearing and a keen sense of smell. They move quietly through the rain forest, becoming most active at night. Wild cats are always hard to spot, in spite of their size, because their markings give them excellent camouflage.

Tiger
A tiger is the largest and strongest wild cat in the world. The tiger is also the only wild cat with a striped coat. A tiger lives on its own and hunts large animals like deer and even baby elephants.

Ocelot

An ocelot climbs trees and sleeps in tree hollows, but it usually prefers to hunt on the ground. The ocelot coat patterning varies from one ocelot to another and no two ocelots have the same markings.

Leopard

A leopard can be spotted or plain black. The black leopard is rare. It was first called a black panther because of its dark coat.

Jaguar

A jaguar will often live close to rivers. A jaguar is a good swimmer and may catch fish, turtles and **caimans** in the water. Young jaguars will stay with their mother for up to two years, while she teaches them to hunt.

THE ELEPHANT AND THE MANATEE

Although it may seem strange, Asian elephants and Amazonian manatees are closely related to each other! Asian elephants have smaller tusks and ears than elephants that live in Africa. Some tame Asian elephants are still used today to help people move timber out of the forests. Amazonian manatees are found in the River Amazon in South America. Manatees spend their whole lives in water.

Asian elephant
There are only about 50,000 of these elephants left, due to their homeland being cut down.

Amazonian manatee
A manatee lives in rivers and eats aquatic plants. It communicates with other manatees underwater, using high-pitched squeaks.

MARMOSETS AND MONKEYS

Having a long tail is very useful for most monkeys and **marmosets**. A monkey's tail is like an extra arm or leg, helping a monkey to hang on a branch as it jumps and swings through the rain forest canopy. But, even so, accidents do happen and occasionally a monkey may fall and injure itself. Youngsters are most likely to get hurt.

Howler monkey
A howler monkey screeches so loudly that its call can be heard over three kilometres away.

Spider monkey
A spider monkey is one of the most acrobatic monkeys. It can use its tail to pick fruit.

Golden lion marmoset
The silky golden marmoset's mane looks like a lion's mane. The marmoset lives in Brazil.

APES

This group includes our closest living relatives in the animal kingdom. The great apes are the gorillas, chimpanzees and orangutans. The gibbons are known as lesser apes. All apes live in family groups. They have powerful arms and expressive faces, but they cannot walk on two legs for any distance.

● Gorilla

The plant-eating gorilla is the largest of all apes. Gorillas talk to each other using noises and gestures. The gorilla lives on the ground and sleeps in its forest floor nest.

Orangutan
Sometimes called the 'old man of the woods', the orangutan is more solitary than other apes. Its long, powerful arms and weak legs make the orangutan more at home in the trees than on the ground.

Gibbon
The smallest and most active ape. It lives high up in the treetops.

Chimpanzee
A chimp eats fruit and vegetables, and will hunt for insects and birds' eggs. A chimp may also kill small animals.

RAIN FOREST PEOPLE

Many different groups of people live in the world's rain forests. They are **hunter-gatherers**. Until recently the forest provided all their needs – food, shelter, medicine and clothes. But now their way of life has been disrupted as people from cities have cleared large areas of forest.

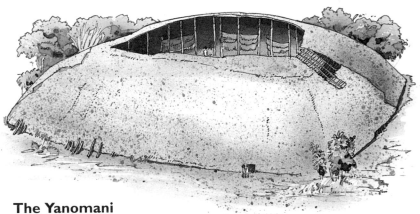

The Yanomani
The Amerindians in Brazil live together in a large, round building called a **yano**.

The Penan
Some Penan people still live in the traditional way in the forests of Sarawak, which is part of Malaysia. The Penan hunt animals by creeping up on them and firing poisonous darts from their blowpipes. They also gather plants and fruit. The Penan build their homes out of branches, logs and plants. They use forest plants for medicines.

VANISHING RAIN FORESTS

An area of rain forest the size of a football pitch is being cut down every second of every day. The wood from the trees is being sold and the land is used for farming or mining. This means that the homes of rain forest people, animals and plants are being destroyed for ever. Some **species** have almost certainly become extinct because of forest clearance, before we even knew they existed.

Bird of paradise

Some of the most unusual animals live in rain forests. This bird of paradise is called Wallace's standard wing. It is found on just two Indonesian islands. If it loses its forest home, there will be nowhere else for it to live.

Gone forever

Roads slash through vast areas of former forest. In **deforested** areas, the thin soil covering will blow or wash away in the rain.

AMAZING RAIN FOREST FACTS

- **Largest rain forest** Amazonia is the world's largest area of rain forest. It covers an area of six-and-a-half million square kilometres, which is larger than the whole of Western Europe.

- **Poisonous birds** The first known poisonous birds were discovered in the rain forests of Papua New Guinea in 1992. Hooded pitohuis produce a poison which is similar to that of the poison arrow frogs.

- **Big leaps** Gibbons can leap over ten metres from one tree to another without falling, which is about the same as three cars lined up end-to-end.

- **Big and poisonous** King cobras are the biggest poisonous snakes in the world. Living in Asia, they can grow to a length of nearly six metres.

- **Slowest mammals** Three-toed sloths, which live in the rain forests of South America, are the slowest of all mammals. They move, on the ground, at about two metres per minute.

- **Deadliest spiders** The most deadly spiders in the world live in the rain forests of Brazil. They often hide in shoes and clothes.

- **Killer frogs** Poison arrow frogs can each produce enough poison to kill fifty people.

- **Endangered** The golden lion marmoset is a highly endangered animal. This is because of the destruction of its rain forest homeland.

GLOSSARY

Amphibian A cold-blooded animal which lives on land and in water. Frogs and toads are amphibians.

Caiman A type of crocodile which lives in Central and South America. Unfortunately its skin is often used to make handbags.

Camouflage The way in which an animal hides itself, using its body shape or colour to blend into the background.

Canopy The tallest layer of trees in the rain forest.

Carnivorous An animal which feeds on meat or fish.

Deforest To cut down trees in such large numbers that the forest eventually disappears.

Fin The limb of a fish, used for swimming.

Hover To fly without moving forwards or backwards.

Hunter-gatherers People who live by hunting animals and gathering food.

Marmoset A long-tailed monkey, living in South and Central America. They have silky fur and sharp claws.

Nutrients Foodstuffs which are necessary for life.

Predator An animal which hunts other animals.

Reptile A cold-blooded animal with a scaly skin, such as a crocodile, lizard, tortoise or snake.

Rodent A small mammal characterised by its sharp front teeth.

Sandbank A raised area of sand on the river bottom, which can become exposed when the water level is low.

Shoal A large group of fish.

Spawn Fish or amphibians producing eggs.

Species A group of animals which are related to one another and which only breed within their own kind.

Tropics The hottest part of the world, around the Equator.

Understorey The lower level of the rain forest, beneath the canopy.

Vapour A gas in the atmosphere.

Weevil A type of beetle, with quite a small head and a large body.

Yano The name of the building built as a home by the Yanomani people in Brazil.

INDEX *(Entries in **bold** refer to an illustration)*